FREE BONUS

EASY FOOD & WINE PAIRING TECHNIQUES

After discovering your new favorites while unlocking your palate, you may be curious about pairing these new gems with cuisine.

I've set up a free bonus as an easy guide to start your practice with food and wine pairing.

You can access that at:
www.LauraMasterSomm.com/Bonus

UNLOCK YOUR PALATE:

HOW TO TASTE WINE, IMPRESS YOUR FRIENDS AND BECOME A WINE PRO

By Laura Williamson

Laura Williamson

ISBN 13: 978-1719829458

DEDICATION

This is dedicated to all wine lovers...

...those who allow wine to enhance their life, ushering in deep joy from the eternal quest to uncover unknown wines and unlock their palate via their journey.

TABLE OF CONTENTS

CHAPTER 1
OUR MISSION

If I had a dollar for every time a client asked me what my favorite wine was, I'd be globetrotting carefree around the world right now.

My usual response is to return their question to them, asking how they would select a favorite among their children? They chuckle, then wait again for my answer, to which I try and explain my favorites are very individual and shift as a direct relation of my current mood, or my potential dinner plans, or the weather at the time and a whole host of additional, somewhat trivial but personally perfunctory, reasons.

My aim is to instill in them the notion that despite my favorites, which they may or may not like, they too have very worthy preferences, which hold far greater significance than my personal choices.

Next, I attempt to go to great links to convince clients that becoming their own critic is not only possible, but also relatively easy with practice, and that deep empowerment can result, further boosting self-confidence with just achieving a basic grasp of wine structure.

If I could do it, anyone can. I say this because I was born and raised in a dry county in Arkansas and never encountered wine until college. I became curious about it once I witnessed the power it garnered over conversation at the dinner table. I quickly realized fluency in wine was a skill that could manifest on many levels and set out to learn basics to support my needs.

This journey to understanding personal preference for wines, including styles, regions, grapes and producers, can be both fun and exciting, simply because this learning process is built around practice. Now who doesn't want to practice sharpening their wine tasting skills?

If your curiosity lured you to this, then chances are you will embrace the focus this endeavor requires and look forward to the needed practice that will guide your journey.

The old saying "practice makes perfect" has roots of 500+ years, and for good reason, as it is no surprise you become better at what you do through repetition. Sometimes, I just love this saying because it helps me justify my need to continue the journey of sourcing new wines to further the quest of deciphering my palate.

You wouldn't think a Master Sommelier would feel a need to justify this *practice*, since it is a profession, but tasting wine and discovering new grapes, styles, regions and producers is such a rewarding, fulfilling endeavor. But there are times I catch myself feeling a bit guilty from loving the practice as much as I do.

The greater the practice, the deeper the capacity to expand beyond your normal steadfast comfort zone where it is far too easy to choose the same wine every day, or the same three wines every week, without even thinking about it.

Decoding your palate will be an adventure, and a rewarding endeavor at that, and no sooner than once you begin this practice, will you realize how surprised you have become with your ability to learn and appreciate varied wine styles and grapes you never dreamed possible.

To launch this endeavor, you must bring an open mind, a love for wine and a desire to shake off uneasiness around what you have not yet learned.

One last promise and guarantee: after embarking on this process, your palate will begin to shift and continue shifting as long as you carry out the practice. The journey will not end, unless of course you stop practicing. So be ready to embrace *you* along with all the shifts you will experience, as the depth and magnitude of those changes is uncertain, but the fact that you will certainly change, is not.

This will be FUN, so let's get started...

CHAPTER 2
THE PROCESS

Our mission is to evaluate and dissect the key sectors that impact the roadmap to personal preference. The fine-tuning of this process will provide a better grasp of the reasoning behind our individual choices and aid in supporting growth beyond our comfortable, safe, go-to wine favorites.

The most basic key sectors that impact preference correlate to wine structure. There are many factors beyond the basic four we will contemplate, but by simplifying our approach, we ease the analysis of a complex subject. Therefore, we will limit our focus to the nature of fruit, acidity, alcohol/body and tannin as it relates to wine.

Once these factors have been mastered, you can intensify the analysis procedure by expanding your scope to include texture, balance, length of finish, complexity, and potential for aging, but this broadening is not paramount to capturing an introductory summation for qualifying tendencies toward personal preferences in wine. The extended analysis merely creates a fuller assessment. However, while the learning process is just beginning, simplifying the focus develops more focused precision and fosters more confident results.

CHAPTER 3
NATURE OF FRUIT

We start our process by evaluating the nature or style of fruit. By nature of fruit, I mean intensity, condition and how these semantics impact the overall persona of the wine.

Is the fruit juicy, opulent, plump, oozing, the absolute main/only feature of the wine? Or in contrast, is the fruit more restrained, tart, barely ripe, angular, racy, or even baked or dried allowing more layers to unfold in the wine beyond just decadent, ripe fruit?

Your preference for either of these angles is quite defining and can be fairly definitive regarding personal style and desire for wines that are either fruit-driven or not.

Warmer climates will yield riper, more unctuous fruit while cooler climates produce the opposite. This concept is quite intuitive by understanding that higher sugar accumulation is possible in grapes sourced from warm, sun-soaked regions, versus the opposite coming from cooler, growth-challenged ripening zones.

7

Fermentation of wine is a simple process: existing yeast devour grape sugar and in part create alcohol and CO_2. If riper fruit exists for yeast to consume, then more times than not, the final wine will reflect this power of ripeness from the harvested grapes. Thus it makes sense to conclude that where more sun is present, higher sugar levels will result and plush, decadent, obvious fruit in the wine will be the end characteristic, dominating the style.

Many warmer climate wine producing zones occur in the USA, South America, Australia, Spain, Portugal and Southern Rhone where blacker berried, sweeter almost jam-like fruit descriptors are in sync when used as a tasting note for red wines from these origins. For richer white wines, weightier tropical fruit nuance is common but a more exaggerated, concentrated palate feel can result too if the condition of the fruit is of a dehydrated, candied or baked nature. If you enjoy wines from these areas, most likely your preference is geared toward the lush, easy, fruit-forward charm of wines originating in regions where sun is ample.

In contrast, cooler, more northerly lying vineyards with potentially higher altitude, coastal fog (also known as the marine layer), humidity, large diurnal daily temperature swings (difference between daytime high and nighttime low) or even rain usually lead to more restrained wines, possibly austere in some of the coolest vintages, where fruit might be lacking, or when present, remains tart, zippy, lifted and electric due to compromised or challenged ripening. If this ideal of a tarter, red-berried fruit as the backbone for red wines or green apple skin and lemon for whites resonates within you, a preference for cooler zones resulting in less sugar accumulation coupled with mineral, earthy drive supports your preference.

These cooler wine zones are found in the northern parallels of USA and Europe, southern parallels in New Zealand, South America and South Africa as well as hillside vineyards or mountains and coastal areas.

We haven't yet factored in age to a wine and how age impacts fruit, but as wines mature, youthful, simple fruit begins to shed, like a toddler shedding baby fat, and evolve into a complex, delineated style due to a conversion to the condition of the fruit. This is most noticeably displayed on the palate as transformation from juicy, ripe fruit to dried, baked or even cooked fruit.

For most wines produced globally, this conversion to a developed style from a youthful new-vintage release requires merely a couple years rather than decades, though a tiny percent of world production fosters extraordinary wines which can easily require 20+ years for the fruit and the wine to evolve.

But, when evaluating the fruit of a wine you prefer, it is imperative not only to analyze the style of the fruit, but also assess the condition of the fruit and contemplate whether this condition resulted due to the maturity of the wine or is rather a direct reflection of the origin and growing conditions in which the fruit was sourced.

CHAPTER 4
PRESENCE OF ACIDITY

The next critical measure to arriving at our desired style is to determine the impact of acidity within the wine, including its relation to the overall essence of the wine, and then extrapolate how our personal preference for either less or more acid weaves into the full desire framework.

If we follow our warm versus cool climate analogy, keeping in mind the basic principle that sugar accumulation is inversely related to presence of total acid, we can then fairly easily surmise and conclude on our preference for acidity.

Warmer growing regions around the world have faster ripening vineyards, and in turn, fruit that loses acidity after a threshold of concentration of sugars has occurred. In many of these warm to hot zones, growers are forced to actually add some acid back into the fermenting must in an attempt to balance the ripe fruit. This is done in a fairly natural manner by adding tartaric acid (cream of tartar as it is known in cooking/baking) back into the grape must as a tool for balancing the final wine. By doing this, a winemaker will lift the intensity of the fruit to avoid any cloying feeling resulting on the palate from riper grapes.

Cooler growing areas in contrast to warmer regions usually battle the opposite outcome: too little ripeness, or inclement weather arriving prior to full ripeness of fruit, so that resulting wines tend to be more direct, pointed, angular and nervous as a function of the acid shining brighter than the ripeness of fruit.

This explanation is a simplified version of the complex total underlying mechanisms previously mentioned, but for our journey, we merely need to evaluate whether we prefer more supple, round, creamy, weighty wines (that reflect greater sugar accumulation and thus less acidity) or if we desire more transparent, crystalline, filigreed styles that reflect mineral tension in lieu of fruit drive.

You can always sense the intensity of acidity by noting the degree to which you salivate after sipping a wine: if your mouth waters easily and this sensation drives the finish, most likely the wine has elevated acidity. And if you love this style and appreciate the zippy, deft feel on your palate, chances are you prefer a wine backed by more acidity rather than less.

In some cases, ripe, fruit-driven wines can surprisingly have firm acidity. Most likely this unexpected contrast prevailed because the winemaker set out to balance concentrated fruit by adding acid, but misjudged the necessary adjustment, resulting in a wine with juxtaposed concentration of sugar against higher than needed acidity. Despite this being a confusing outome and style, sense can be made when remembering winemakers continually work to improve upon Mother Nature, and in doing so work to craft as balanced a style as possible to offer consumers not only a sound product, but the best product achievable under the circumstances in which they manage. And though perfection is their quest, their interpretation of perfection and how it relates to the wine they fashion is linked to *their preference* or to their expectation of the market's preference in which they are selling.

CHAPTER 5

ALCOHOL AND DENSITY

P reference for body, density or weight as it relates to the power of wine provides another stylistic measure that contributes to our desired palate.

To recap, full-bodied, heavier wines tend to originate from warmer, sun-drenched zones and produce riper fruit, with less acidity. The opposite holds true for lighter body wines hailing from cooler areas yielding more delicate fruit and higher acidity.

Weight or density in wine is closely linked to percentage of alcohol. A quick review of the simple fermentation equation makes this concept easy to grasp:

$$Sugar + yeast = wine \& CO_2$$

With higher levels of sugar in harvested fruit, the yeast devour all sugar present, converting this ripeness to alcohol (and CO_2). Therefore, riper, juicier fruit will result in higher alcohol wines with richer body, denser weight and more power-packed intensity.

Those who crave more decadent, heavy, strong or even massive wines, do so more often than not because they love the feel on the palate, and in many cases, perceive this density to correlate directly to higher quality.

Early famous wine critics also fostered this notion that more power-driven, higher alcohol wines supported finer quality, as most derived their direct knowledge of this belief from painful reality. Their initial evaluations of the great wines from France and Italy harkened back to a plethora of challenging, stark vintages throughout the '60s and '70s. With global warming revving by the mid-'90s, the wine idsutry has been a proud recipient of a constant stream of warm, easy-ripening vintages that many consumers have grown accustomed to and now become dependent upon. But it is paramount to remember: power-packed wines do not automatically render superlative quality.

After studying vintages going back to the early 1900s, tasting enough wines to yield confidence discussing vintages from 1945 on and cellaring my personal wine collection beyond twenty years, I can state with certainty that paying attention to less-touted, minimally hyped vintages from more classic years can offer affordable and in many cases age-worthy alternatives to the blockbuster, critic-boosted legendary vintages that pack a hefty price.

Classic, cool-toned vintages can produce elegant, refined wines exuding more balanced alcohol, elevated acid, and a more harmonious, stealth-like, nimble capacity to age. There are in rare occurrences particular vintages that should be avoided all together, but these are easy to research with wines difficult to find since compromised output results from disastrous weather.

Many serious wine collectors will be the first to admit that bold intense vintages truly produce enjoyable wines, but the greatest surprises often reflect challenging, less-regarded or misunderstood vintages. Collectors have learned to rely on their palate and preference but use critics' opionions to help navigate more easily their preference rather than holding popular critic opinions as the holy grail.

CHAPTER 6
TANNIN AND GRIP

L ast but not least, an understanding of tannin structure, the persona around different sources of tannin in wine, and how this is revealed on the palate, provides the final link to steering preference toward favorite wine styles.

If the term "tannin" feels like a new concept, a more simple analogy regarding a different common source for tannin apart from wine can ease clarity in understanding this concept. If you have ever steeped black tea too long without softening it through addition of sugar or milk, chances are you experienced a drying sensation along your gums that also felt bitter and astringent. This sensation is caused by tannin, and it acts very similarly in black tea, fostering a bitter, astringent taste that simultaneously dries the gums and mouth as it does so in wine.

Most discussions relating to tannin hark back to red wine, even though it is possible, but much less common, to experience mild tannin in white wine, as the most prolific sources of tannin come from seeds, stems, and skins of grapes, including red and white grapes.

Additionally, since tannin is plant-derived, oak used within the winemaking process provides another source. This extends to oak barrels used either during the fermentation process or also during élevage (the process of aging or maturing the wine), and further links to the intensity of the toasting or charring (cooperage) used in the barrel making process.

Tannins from seeds and stems can be the most poignant, and a little goes a long way for the majority of red grapes, as many times these sources can be harsh, overpowering the wine and detracting from it. Stems can be included in a fermenting must or pre-soak to extend an earthy character in red wines, and this practice is more commonly used for specific red grapes, such as with Pinot Noir in Burgundy, where ripe stems (not inclusion of under-ripe stems) add layers of nuance to the overall wine.

None of the previous discussion is too critical to our understanding other than a grasp of the notion that concentration of tannin will shift based on the source, and a preference for types of tannin can be traced back to wines, grapes and production styles.

For instance, we can analyze two different grapes both known to possess high tannins on many occasions. The Nebbiolo grape of the famed Barolo and Barbaresco appellations in Piedmont, Italy, is widely accepted as a high-tannin varietal, but many times those tannins feel silky and elegant across the palate versus the chunkier, more foursquare grip that tannins from Cabernet Sauvignon can exude. So even though both grapes can result in high tannins, the manner in which those tannins are experienced on the palate can impact our palate very differently and in turn sway our preference.

Types of oak barrels can also impact the way tannins are revealed on the palate. Though technology drives advancement within cooperage, variations can still be perceived by experts, and American oak is known to have a bit more grip than French oak, versus use of oak chips or oak powder that can feel even harsh (but keeps cost down in lieu of expensive barrels).

As red wines mature, tannins precipate out as sediment. This explains the reason behind cellaring wines with firm, aggressive tannins to allow time to turn the texture of those tannins into a more silky, velvety feel. This is also the reason why mature wines are decanted, to skillfully remove sediment (denatured tannins) without shaking it, because once stirred, sediment acts like a gauze over the wine, masking the full resonance and stifling the expression.

Historically, many wines required cellaring to allow chewy tannins to relax. Today, modern technology has gifted winemakers access to numerous tools and tricks that help ensure plush, juicy, easy-drinking styles that not only eliminate the need for cellaring but also diminish the benefit to this process. As a result, the majority of red wine production today is supple in style, ready for immediate consumption and best when enjoyed within 3-5 years of release.

Determining your preference for the power of tannin, as well as the style of tannin, is an important pathway to understanding whether a fondness exists for chewy, grippy wines or an inclination toward a more satiny, seamless feel influences your partiality.

CHAPTER 7

SYNERGIZING STRUCTURE

Once the aforementioned aspects impacting structure have been studied and familiarity anchored via practice, the passageway to personal preference will become succinct and evident, but also ever-changing, as this discovery is expansionary, not static.

Once you coin your preference, you are then free to experiment by sampling similar wines from lesser known grapes and regions around the world.

Your courage to broaden your universe through seeking new discoveries is the precursor to impressing your friends and becoming a self-made wine pro. The more you let your curiousity guide you, the more fascinating your wine exploration becomes.

Soon, if you pay attention, you will begin to realize your personal preference and whether it points to Old World wines, possibly with higher acidity and more moderate alcohol with a predisposition for earthy, mineral-laced attributes where fruit is subdued rather than New World counterparts with moderate acidity, higher alcohol, glossy oak and opulent fruit that prevails over earthy nuance. Neither is better than the other but merely a preference versus a competition. And once you own your preference and understand your predilection for it, magic in the realm of wine starts to unfold.

Let some of these below metioned hidden gems help launch your path to impressing your friends and support your growth while stepping into your new wine pro persona.

Remember to keep track of both your favorites and those that fall short as this detail will be beneficial for tools mentioned toward the end of the book.

Excellent but lesser-known rich and voluptuous black-fruited red wines include:

- blends from Priorat, Spain
- blends from Douro, Portugal
- blends from Roussillon, France
- Primitivo from Apulia, Italy
- Cabernet Sauvignon from Goriska, Brda, Slovenia
- Agiorgitiko from Nemea, Greece

- Lemberger from Wurttemberg, Germany
- Blaufrankisch from Burgenland, Austria
- Shiraz or Grenache from Clare Valley, South Australia
- Syrah or Cabernet Sauvignon from Margaret River, Western Australia
- Cabernet Sauvignon from Coonawarra, South Australia

Many elegant, silky, red-fruit driven red wines exist as alternatives to Pinot Noir from Burgundy and USA:

- Pinot Noir from Franken, Germany
- Pinot Noir from Central Otago, New Zealand
- Pinot Noir from Patagonia, Argentina
- Gamay from Beaujolais, France
- Valpolicella from Veneto, Italy
- Nebbiolo from Barolo in Piedmont, Italy
- Sangiovese from Chianti in Tuscany, Italy
- Xinomavro from Northern Greece
- St Laurent from Burgenland, Austria
- Zweigelt from Burgenland, Austria

The same exploratory options exist for white wines, and intriguing, slightly esoteric fuller bodied whites include:

- Friulano from Friuli, Italy
- Rebula from Goriska Brda, Slovenia
- Greco di Tufo from Campania, Italy
- Falanghina from Campania, Italy
- Verdicchio from Marche, Italy
- Malagousia from Epanomi, Greece
- blends from Hermitage in N Rhone, France

This above list is especially important for you if your wheelhouse is Chardonnay more because you love the creamy texture it exudes rather than the toasty oak that can accompany it. The above list is rarely linked to oak, but definitely decadent in weight from concentrated fruit grown on unique soils.

And if you are searching for substitutes for lighter, more vibrant whites, these are great:

- Muscadet from Loire Valley, France
- Arinto from Bucelas, Portugal
- Albarino from Rias Baixas, Spain

- Silvaner from Franken, Germany
- Gruner Veltliner from Kamptal, Austria
- Semillon from Hunter Valley, Australia
- Riesling (dry) from Nahe, Germany
- Riesling (dry) from Wachau, Austria
- Pigato from Liguria, Italy
- blends from Sicily, Italy
- Assyrtiko from Santorini, Greece
- Pinot Blanc from Pfalz, Germany

These twists from the norm offer a unique approach, helping to steer your path of discovery with confidence while accessing the unknown based on your newly discovered preferences for wine.

Where possible, put these lists to the test, even taking the list to your favorite wine shop and pointing to it to eliminate stress involved with mispronunciation. A great wine shop will be able to steer you in a similar direction should none of the recommendations be available. Additionally, searching the internet for these grapes and appellations linked to production prior to visiting your shop will help streamline your purchasing by providing insight into average bottle costs before you even check availability at your local store.

CHAPTER 8

TOOLS FOR LEARNING

As we wind down the platform for this guide, reflecting on knowledge gained deciphering wine structure as well as the blueprint for seeking out more esoteric choices, one final tool can also catapult your personal path to becoming a wine pro. This last tool is a wine app supported by Artificial Intelligence.

You might be asking, why Artificial Intelligence? Especially if we are relying on ourselves to prompt our forward movement with learning, but computers and software can work in tendem with our process and actually propel our endeavor and magnify our efforts.

Nowhere else is it more evident than the revolutionary app originally called Wine Ring, but now known as RingIt. This app can start to work for you, guiding your preferences, with only a few selection preferences entered. When you are curious about how you might react to a new wine, just enter the selection then let the app respond, taking into account your personal profile, how likely you are to enjoy it or not. The app will also encourage you to try unknown wines by offering suggestions aligned with your profile. The app will even prompt you in the opposite manner when necessary if you choose a wine not synchronized with your previously recorded preferences.

Again, this is possible because the app starts to work and decode your desires after just 3 wines are entered into it. The more you record your preferences, the more the app constructs your exact profile, advising you on the outcome of liking an unknown wine or not before you even try it (or buy it).

Loading selections into the app is as easy as taking a picture and rating the wine if you have tasted it, or if you are assessing whether you should try or buy it, you enter the wine and the app states the expected outcome for a requested selection as a result of your profile and the algorithms linked to your personal preference.

Many worry this extraordinary tool might replace the sommelier, however, I personally embrace it because I feel when consumers are guided more succinctly to what they love, with confidence to try unique, esoteric wines, their passion grows too. This expansion within consumers eventually guides them back to sommelier assistance, which will always surpass even the most specialized computer platform due to the simple fact of enhanced interaction with human communication.

I know this tool will help carry forward fast learning and discovery, so embrace it and watch magic unfold.

FREE BONUS

EASY FOOD & WINE PAIRING TECHNIQUES

After discovering your new favorites while unlocking your palate, you may be curious about pairing these new gems with cuisine.

I've set up a free bonus as an easy guide to start your practice with food and wine pairing.

You can access that at:
www.LauraMasterSomm.com/Bonus

Printed in Great Britain
by Amazon